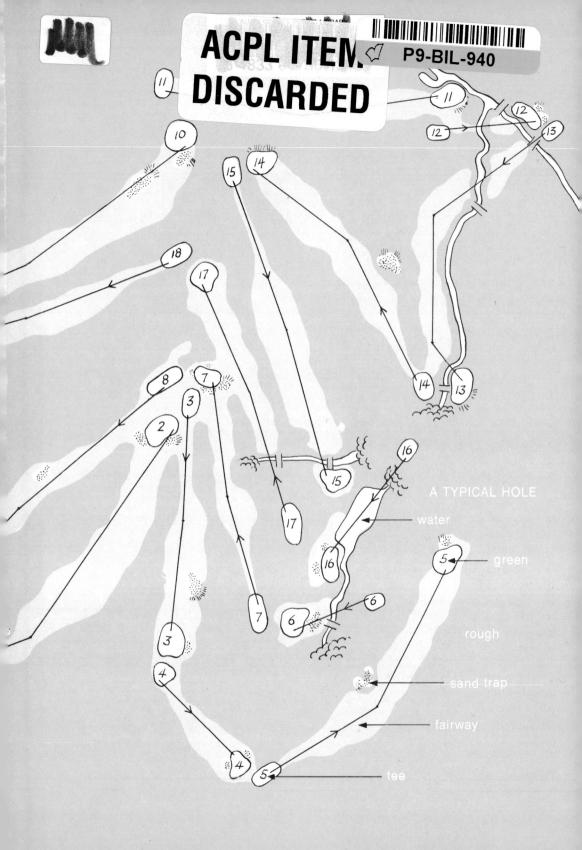

A TYPICAL HOLE

water

green

rough

sand trap

fairway

tee

Sports Consultant:
COLONEL RED REEDER
Former Member of the West Point Coaching Staff
and Special Assistant to the West Point
Director of Athletics

GOLFING GREATS

TWO TOP PROS

•

BY GUERNSEY VAN RIPER, JR.

GARRARD PUBLISHING COMPANY
CHAMPAIGN, ILLINOIS

Library of Congress Cataloging in Publication Data

Van Riper, Guernsey, 1909–
    Golfing greats: two top pros.

    SUMMARY: Sketches the golfing careers of two of the
game's pros, Jack Nicklaus and Lee Trevino.

    1. Nicklaus, Jack—Juvenile literature. 2. Trevino,
Lee—Juvenile literature. 3. Golf—Juvenile literature.
[1. Nicklaus, Jack. 2. Trevino, Lee. 3. Golf—Biog-
raphy] I. Title.
GV964.N5V36   796.352′092′2 [B] [920]   74-16266
ISBN 0-8116-6669-7

Photo credits:

Walter Iooss, Jr.: p. 94
Leonard Kamsler: pp. 6, 30 (all), 58, 71 (all), 74
United Press International: pp. 2, 14, 19, 27, 36, 37, 51, 63,
    64, 79 (both), 82, 89, jacket
Wide World: pp. 5, 10-11, 41, 44, 47, 50 (both), 53, 54, 75, 84

Contents

A powerful swing and a high straight drive
down the fairway by Lee Trevino.

Golf Fever

Anybody can play golf. Kids of ten, men of eighty, and even people with physical handicaps enjoy hitting the little white ball. Why? Because it is fun—and a challenge. It is a game that will last a lifetime.

Golf was born on the windy hills of Scotland around 1400. The first balls were leather covers stuffed with feathers. They were hit with wooden clubs with strange names like "baffing spoon," "cleek," and "niblick."

It was not until four hundred years later that the game moved across the ocean to America. On Washington's Birthday in 1888,

John Reid and his friends played the first game of golf in the United States in a cow pasture in Yonkers, New York. Golf fever spread quickly throughout America. Today there are millions of players and more than 10,000 golf courses.

The Scots invented golf but Americans lost no time improving it. They replaced the "featheries" with a lively rubber ball that can travel 130 miles per hour. Another invention was a wooden peg, called a tee, that held the ball off the ground and made it easier to hit. Americans added their own words to the sport. One day a golfer's ball bounced off a bird, and he finished the hole in one shot less than normal. He called it a "birdie." The name caught on, and soon everyone called a one under par score a "birdie;" a two under par became an "eagle." Americans added style too. One Texas millionaire played a round of golf by flying from hole to hole in his own helicopter!

In the beginning the game was simple. There were only thirteen rules. As golf became more popular there were many arguments about what the rules meant. So in 1894 the United States Golf Association was formed. It makes the rules. It sets handicaps. It decides whether new equipment will be allowed or not, and it conducts tournaments.

Tournaments are for the best players. In the United States there are three kinds of tournaments: amateur, professional, and open. "Open" means that both professional and amateurs can enter. Amateurs cannot win money prizes, but they hope to win or make a good score in these important events.

There are four major tournaments for amateurs. They are the United States Open, the United States Amateur, the British Open, and the British Amateur. To win them all in one year is called a Grand Slam. Only one

Pro golfing has its tense moments—this one provided by Jack Nicklaus.

man, the great Bobby Jones, has ever done it. Since his smashing victory in 1930, no one has even come close.

For professional golfers there are four tournaments that make up the Professional Grand Slam. They are the United States Open, the British Open, the Masters, and the Professional Golfers Association (P.G.A.). So

far no one has scored a Pro Grand Slam. It is the dream of every serious golfer. Today tournament golf is dominated by professionals. There is big money to be won. Some pros have earned more than a million dollars playing golf.

Consistency is what counts on the professional circuit. In most of the 45 tournaments for professionals, only 144 players are allowed to enter. After two rounds, half the players are cut and cannot play the last two rounds and compete for the money prizes. The winners are those who play consistently good golf for four long rounds.

Golf champions are not alike. Some are shy and quiet. Others are colorful and talkative, with a huge army of fans. Some are icy cool, always in charge. Others lose their tempers. They throw their clubs into a lake or stomp on their hats.

On the courses they jokingly call "Green Monster" and "Heartbreak Hills," these men wear lucky shirts, carry rabbits' feet, or use only one putter they think will bring them luck. But these are not the things that make a champion at such a difficult game.

The qualities that set these great champions apart from other players are judgment, control, courage, and ability to

12

concentrate. A golfer must be able to do more than hit. He must be able to think. Golf is a power game but a great player must have nerves of steel. He must keep his mind on the game in spite of the TV cameras, the thousands of spectators, and the other golfers around him.

The secrets of winning golf are found in these stories of super golfers Jack Nicklaus and Lee Trevino. Their lives show the very different ways two men have reached the top in golf.

Jack Nicklaus
The Golden Bear

"There's going to be some great golf played today!" exclaimed a spectator at the 1965 Masters golf tournament.

"I can hardly wait to see who will get the lead," said his companion.

The third round of the important Masters tournament was about to begin. Only the best professionals and amateurs are invited to play in this event. Never had so many people crowded onto the Augusta National golf course at Augusta, Georgia. Some of the world's greatest golfers had played sparkling golf in the first two rounds on the beautiful, tree-lined course. And the fans were eager to see the next round.

On the big scoreboard, the lowest score was 138. That score appeared beside three names—there was a three-way tie!

One of the three was Arnold Palmer, the popular American champion who had already won the Masters tournament four times. The fans loved Arnie, and many thought he would win.

Then there was Gary Player, the South African champion who had won the Masters once. Short but muscular, Player had demonstrated his golfing skill all over the world.

The third and youngest player was Jack Nicklaus (pronounced *Nick*-lus). Jack was only 25, but he had already shown that he could become a superstar. Golf fans were awed by the power of his game. The husky six-footer weighed 210 pounds, and he put all his size and strength behind his power-ful drives.

Jack was ambitious. He had made up his mind to win this Masters tournament. He also wanted to become the greatest golfer who ever lived. On this April day in Augusta, he looked like the greatest.

When Jack stepped to the first tee, the eager crowds lining the course were talking excitedly.

"Who will break the tie today?" was the big question on their minds. The fans leaned forward to get a good view. Then they were silent as Jack prepared to drive.

Jack put every ounce of power into his swing as he drove off the first tee.

There was an "Aaah!" from the crowd as the ball shot out so high and far it nearly disappeared from sight. But there it was! It was right in the fairway, an unbelievable 320 yards away.

Big Jack looked very serious and determined, but he nodded to the crowd as they applauded. He strode off down the fairway, thinking about his next shot. His ball was only a short distance from the green. His next shot showed that he had a delicate touch, for he lofted his ball easily onto the green with an iron club.

On the green he stroked his first putt close —oh, so close—to the cup. He tapped in his second putt easily. Jack had his par four on the first hole. If a golfer does not go over par, he's good. To be a winner, though, he often has to score *under* par.

On the second hole, Jack was in trouble for the only time that day. His long drive was a little to the right. His ball landed in the pine trees beside the fairway.

Jack looked over the situation carefully. He saw an opening in the trees and hit a low shot right through onto the fairway.

Twenty-five-year-old Jack Nicklaus made golf history with his outstanding performance in the 1965 Masters tournament.

His third shot landed on the green. Then he rolled his first putt into the cup for a birdie—one stroke under par. He had scored four on a par five hole.

From then on Jack could not be stopped. His shots were straight and true. Hole after hole he put his ball close to the cup. He had several easy putts for birdies, and some hard ones. While playing the eighteen holes he made eight birdies to score a 64 against par 72.

It was the best score made on the course in 25 years. His three-round total was a new record low at 202.

"They'll never catch him now!" said one of Jack's admirers.

The others tried. Gary Player did well to score a 69, but he was now five strokes behind at 207.

Arnold Palmer finished in even par 72, so he was now eight strokes behind.

On the last day, big Jack continued to play well. He scored a 69. His four-round total of 271 set a new record for the Masters tournament. He finished nine strokes in front of Player and Palmer.

"Fantastic!" was the way the other golfers described Jack's playing.

"That was the greatest tournament performance in golf history," declared Bobby Jones, the famous amateur champion of the 1920s. Jones had helped establish the Augusta National Golf Club. As its president, he presented Jack Nicklaus with the winner's green coat, the kind of coat worn by the members of the Augusta club.

It was a great moment for Jack. He had always looked up to Bobby Jones. He had tried to model his own career after Bobby's.

Even as a boy, Jack had heard his father talk about the brilliant golf Bobby played. He heard how Bobby had become the most famous golfer in the world. Still, Jack was interested in many other sports and activities before he decided to make golf a career.

Jack Nicklaus was born in Columbus, Ohio, January 21, 1940. Bigger and stronger than most of the boys in his grade at school, he soon began to show natural athletic ability. By the time he entered junior high school he was good at football, basketball, baseball, and track. He was a star on all these teams, but his favorite sport was basketball. At Upper Arlington High School he continued to play outstanding basketball, but he had to drop the other games. He had time for only one other sport—golf. He was a member of the high school team. Gradually he came to like golf the best of all sports.

Jack was ten years old when he first walked around a golf course with his father. "Dad" Nicklaus had been an athlete in his school days. He had studied pharmacy in school and now owned some drugstores. He wanted young Jack to have his chance in athletics, too.

Dad Nicklaus put Jack in a golf class in June 1950. The teacher was Jack Grout. He and young Jack got along very well—so well, in fact, that Grout has been Jack's only teacher throughout his career.

Grout would line up his group of boys and girls. He would get them to swing their clubs together. When Jack showed up he was usually greeted by the other boys. "Hey, Snow White! How many balls are you going to hit today?"

The boys liked to tease Jack about his very blond hair. They also liked to tease him because he never wanted to stop practicing. After the group lessons, Jack often would have a private lesson with Grout. Then he would get a bucket of balls—or two or three—and hit practice shots. He wanted to be sure that he remembered what he had learned. Besides, he really loved to hit golf balls.

Young Jack learned fast. He was still ten years old when he shot a score of 95 for eighteen holes. The next year he shot as low as 81. By the time Jack was twelve he shot a 74. The next year, when he was thirteen, Jack broke through to score a 69. Scoring this low was a real accomplishment for one so young.

By the time he was fifteen, Jack Nicklaus had won the Ohio junior title. That year, 1955, he qualified to enter the United States Amateur tournament. He was the second youngest to do so. Bobby Jones was the only one who had been younger.

It wasn't surprising that Jack began to think he was a pretty good golfer. He became angry when things didn't go the

24

way he wanted. He started to throw his clubs around a bit. His dad soon put a stop to that. He told Jack that anger had no place in golf. Jack didn't need to be told twice. Then, just to be sure his son didn't feel too important, Mr. Nicklaus kept reminding him that his accomplishments were at least a year behind Bobby Jones's performance.

Jack finished high school at seventeen and enrolled at Ohio State University. By now golf was a big part of his life. He was entering and winning tournaments, and he played on the Ohio State team.

How did Jack become a good golfer so quickly? He was a good athlete, he concentrated well, and he was a good learner. Athletic skills are required for golf, especially good muscle control and a good sense of timing. The ability to concentrate is essential. Golf is not a "natural" game;

it must be learned. When Jack began to take lessons, he started to learn a series of correct moves with his feet, ankles, knees, thighs, arms, shoulders, back muscles, hands, and head. He practiced until his hands were sore.

When Jack was nineteen, he won the United States Amateur championship at the Broadmoor golf course in Colorado. As a result of this victory, he became a member of America's Walker Cup team that challenged the British at Muirfield in Scotland. Jack helped the best U.S. amateurs to beat England's best in a thrilling two-day battle. To Jack Nicklaus, this friendly but hard-fought competition was sport at its best.

Jack entered the U.S. Open that year, too. He was nineteen years old. Here he could compete against the best professionals as well as the great amateurs. He

Jack holds his own as a member of the U.S. team at the 1959 Walker Cup matches in Scotland.

was disappointed that he didn't score well enough to be allowed to play the last two rounds. The following year, though, he finished second. Jack shot 282, only two strokes behind the winner, Arnold Palmer. That year he won the individual title in the World Amateur tournament. To do so he made the brilliant score of 269 at one of the most difficult courses in America— at Merion, near Philadelphia, Pennsylvania. That season, he won 29 of the 30 matches he entered.

In the summer following his junior year at college, Jack Nicklaus was married. His wife, Barbara, did not play golf. Still, she understood Jack's ambitions, and she wanted to help him all she could.

By the time Jack was 21, he was one of America's outstanding amateur golfers. He had entered the College of Commerce at Ohio State University in the fall of 1961.

He was studying hard and playing a lot of golf.

At the same time, Jack was earning his living by selling insurance. He had a back-breaking schedule.

Jack began to think seriously about becoming a professional golfer and joining the tournament tour. That way he could drop his insurance business and earn an even better income while he continued to attend school. Golf started to become more popular in the early 1960s, and the earnings possible for a pro golfer started to increase. Jack loved the game, and he was sure he could become an even better golfer if he had more time to practice.

Jack did turn professional at the end of 1961. This meant he could no longer enter amateur competition. He spent most of his time now practicing and preparing to compete for the money prizes.

Nicklaus demonstrates his powerful drive.

Jack was determined to become the best player in the world. He worked at it by day and thought about it by night.

Jack's game was built on three important points drilled into him by his teacher, Jack Grout:

First, *in the successful golf swing, you must hold your head still*. When he practiced his swing, Jack had his hair held firmly by Grout's assistant. Sometimes it was a little painful, but he learned. It took him about two years to master this one point.

Second, *to keep good balance, especially in a long, powerful swing, you must learn to roll your ankles just right*. The left ankle is supposed to roll inward on the backswing, then the right ankle is supposed to roll inward on the downswing. It took Jack four or five years to be sure he had this right. He put in hours of practice. If he hit one bad chip shot, he would hit 400 balls in a three-hour practice session, trying to correct the problem.

Third, *go for distance*. This was a surprising lesson Grout taught Jack. Most teachers tell their players to work for a smooth, accurate swing and not to worry about distance. But Grout wanted Jack to have both accuracy and distance. His method was not to use extra muscle-power. Instead, he taught Jack to swing with a long arc. A young player can stretch and develop his muscles so the club can be taken back high and swung through to a high finish. This swing is difficult, but once learned it is effective. The clubhead meets the ball at greater speed, and the ball goes farther.

Another important lesson Jack learned was the need for self-control. He had to remember not to become angry or forget the important points he had learned when the going was tough.

A great champion has to be able to play his best under all conditions. Jack learned that the real opponents in golf are not the other players but the golf course and one's self. The player must know the course. He cannot lose his concentration. Jack would get so set on remembering the course and thinking about his next shot that he would stare straight ahead with a stern expression. Lots of people thought he was a "sour apple."

As a result the crowds were not too friendly to Jack. He didn't get very many cheers or much applause. Even his fellow players made jokes about him, especially because of the weight he had gained. He might be greeted with, "Hey, Blob-o, let's see that new club of yours." Or he might be called "Ohio Fats" or "Whaleman." He didn't smile too much about such remarks, but he didn't let them bother him, either.

Jack Nicklaus started on the professional tour in 1962. The first winter tournaments each year are played in California beginning in January. Then the tournaments are held in warmer cities from Hawaii through the southern states to Florida.

Jack entered tournament after tournament, always thinking he might win. His booming drives and powerful iron shots drew "oohs" and "aahs" from the spectators, but he just didn't score well. He played in sixteen tournaments without a victory. However, he finished in second place in the new Thunderbird Open in New Jersey, the first tournament to join the Masters in offering at least $100,000 in prize money. He did place high enough in other tournaments to pay his expenses with his winnings.

34

Then came spring and the biggest tournament of all, the United States Open. Jack spent an entire week preparing himself for it. Day after day he studied the tough Oakmont course near Pittsburgh, Pennsylvania. As he played practice rounds, he carefully measured distances on each hole. He wrote down landmarks on a card, so he would know just how far it was to the greens for all the holes. Then he would know what club to use from any place on the hilly course.

When actual play started, Jack was hitting the ball well. After four exciting rounds he had a fine score of 283—and a tie for first place with the popular Arnold Palmer.

For the eighteen-hole play-off, Palmer fans—known as Arnie's Army—arrived in droves. They cheered loudly for their champion. This made Jack Nicklaus even more

Jack used fast chip shots (above) and steady putting (right) to win his first major tournament at the 1962 U.S. Open play-off match.

determined to win. He played a great
game, scoring a one under par 71. It was
the older, more experienced Palmer who
made the mistakes. He slipped to a 74.
Jack Nicklaus was U.S. Open champion at
22 years of age.

Having won his first major tournament,
Jack went on to win two more tournaments
before the year was over. Then he topped
off a good season by winning the first

World Series of Golf, a match among the winners of the four major pro titles of the year. He was third from the top of the money winners for that year. However, golf was now taking so much of his time that Jack had to withdraw from Ohio State.

Not everybody was happy about the arrival of the new star on the golfing scene. Some of the golf writers called him "Fat Jack." In their articles they made fun of him for never smiling and for wearing old, rumpled clothes. Some of the fans even booed him on the course when he beat one of their favorites. Usually Jack was thinking so hard about his golf game he didn't pay attention to the crowds.

When he went to Australia to play in some tournaments, he was given another name. They called him the "Golden Bear" because of his size and his thick, blond hair.

Jack Nicklaus continued to practice day after day, both during the big tournaments and between them. Now that he had won the U.S. Open, he wanted to win the other big ones—the Masters, the P.G.A., and the British Open.

In 1963 Jack's game was so good that he won both the Masters and the P.G.A. In the British Open he came in seventh.

The next year Jack failed to win any of the big ones, but he won four tournaments in the United States and two abroad. He placed high so often, he was the leading money winner in 1964.

In 1965 he startled the sports world with his record-smashing victory in the Masters. The next year he won the Masters again and became the first player to win it two years in a row. The same year he made his fifth try for the British Open title at Muirfield in Scotland.

The weather was windy, the fairways were narrow, and the tall, thick grass on the rough made it hard to find the ball and hit it out. However, Jack turned in a fine performance. He won his first British Open, against the toughest competition.

Now he had won all four of the world's major titles. He began to think of winning them all in one year!

Bobby Jones had scored a tremendous Grand Slam in 1930 of the most important tournaments of that time. He had won the British and American amateur championships plus the British and American open championships, all in that one year. No one had come close to that accomplishment. Could Jack Nicklaus win the Professional Grand Slam of the British and American Opens, plus the Masters and the P.G.A. in one year? That would be the only way he could approach Bobby Jones's record. Jack

Jack hits from the deep rough on the Muirfield, Scotland, golf course during the 1966 British Open competition.

was no longer an amateur. Besides, the Masters and the P.G.A. were now more important than the strictly amateur championships.

While he was thinking about this difficult goal, something happened to Jack's game. His drives began to go astray. His putts would not drop into the cup. The winter and spring of 1967 he was in a long slump.

"Whatever became of Jack Nicklaus?" some of the sportswriters asked.

"It looks as though he's finished," some said when Jack failed to qualify for the last two rounds of the Masters. What could have gone wrong?

With determination, Jack continued on the tournament trail that season. He used every spare moment to work hard on his game. Gradually his swing started to improve. He began to control his drives. He regained his touch on the putting greens. He went back to his earlier style of putting. He used a firmer stroke, with more follow-through to help keep the ball on line.

He found a new putter that felt just right when he hit the ball. The club had a white face. Jack called it "White Fang," and it served him well for a long time.

He felt he was ready when it came time for the U.S. Open at Baltusrol in Springfield, New Jersey.

"Jack is really back!" was the surprised cry around the golf course as the tournament got underway.

On the very difficult Baltusrol course, Jack had magnificent rounds of 71, 67, 72, 65 to set a new U.S. Open record score of 275.

He continued his great play the rest of the season. He finished as top money winner for the year.

For three years Jack continued his strong

Sporting a new image, Nicklaus blasts out of a sand trap in the 1971 P.G.A. championship.

play. He won six tournaments in the United States and several abroad. He finished high on the list of prize-money winners each year, but during the three years he did not win one of the "big" titles. Even so, his determination to be the world's greatest golfer did not change.

Something did change, though. It was Jack himself. He decided to slim down. He lost twenty pounds. He looked better, and he felt better. He started to smile more and to relax more around the crowds.

"Fat Jack" was gone. Instead there was the good-natured "Golden Bear."

When the 1971 tour started Jack's game was going well. He felt he might really make the Grand Slam.

The P.G.A. was the first major title to be won. It was held at Palm Beach Gardens, Florida, the last week in February. Jack prepared himself completely for this first

major test of the year. He took several
weeks off the tour and stayed at his Florida
home. A combination of relaxation and stiff
practice gave his game the edge he wanted.

Jack led the tournament all the way. He
won with a score of 281, seven under par.
Now he had won each of the four major
titles at least twice. Could he win all four in
one year?

For the next major test, the Masters at
Augusta, Georgia, in April, Jack prepared
just as hard as before. Although he got off
to a slow start, he managed to tie for first
place after three rounds. He and Charles
Coody had scores of 209.

On the final round, Jack could not make
his putts drop into the cup for the birdies
he needed to win. He made par 72 and tied
for second. Coody's 70 gave him the championship and the famous green coat of the
Masters winner.

At the 1971 U.S. Open, Jack hits from a sand trap. Lee Trevino (right) leans on his club and waits patiently in the play-off match.

Jack just shook his head. He couldn't have tried harder.

He was still eager for the next major test, the U.S. Open. He was a strong favorite.

His four-round score of 280 at the Merion club in Ardmore, Pennsylvania, was good, but only good enough for a first-place tie. The rising new star, Lee Trevino, scored 280 also.

In the eighteen-hole play-off, Jack took a quick lead at the first hole. Then he ran into trouble in Merion's dangerous sand traps. On the second hole, he took two shots to get out of the sand. At the short third hole his tee shot again went into the sand. His ball was so deep in the sand he could hardly see it. Again, it took him two shots to get out. He was then two strokes behind.

It was a seesaw battle after that, but Jack could never catch up. He finished with a one over par 71 to Trevino's 68.

Even though there was no Grand Slam for Jack that year, he continued to play great golf. He won three other titles and set a new record for money winning for the year. One important writer called Jack Nicklaus the world leader among golfers.

So good was Jack's game that the golf writers began to talk about a possible Grand Slam in 1972.

"What are his chances, about one in a million?" they asked.

Nobody knew the answer to that, but Jack came through with some remarkable performances.

He "warmed up" for the major tests by winning two firsts and two seconds in the early tournaments on the pro tour. For the Masters tournament he put in days of hard practice over the Augusta course that he liked so well. He made a strong start with a 68 the first day. Nobody could catch him after that, although Bruce Crampton, the steady Australian, came close and finished in second place. Jack wound up with a 286 for his fourth Masters victory.

Now he had the first leg on his try for a Grand Slam. The next big tournament was the U.S. Open at the tough Pebble Beach, California, course in June. Again Jack was ready. Again the pressure was

Nicklaus faced grass (left) and sand traps (below and right) on the wet Pebble Beach course at the 1972 U.S. Open.

on him to win, for he was the favorite. With the wind and rain making playing conditions very bad, the leaders' scores were bunched close together after two days. Jack's steady golf the last two rounds put him three strokes in front. Jack had won the U.S. Open for the third time. Again it was Crampton in second place, followed by Palmer and Trevino.

The victory was Jack's thirteenth major title. Bobby Jones had won only thirteen titles in his entire career. Jack was just 32 years old with many playing seasons ahead.

This win gave Jack the second leg on his try for the Grand Slam. Next came the British Open at Muirfield, Scotland, in July. It was here that Jack had won his first British Open in 1966. He knew well the narrow fairways and deep bunkers of the tough seaside course. He arrived early to study the course some more and to practice with the British golf ball, which is a little smaller than the U.S. one. Because it was usually windy and rainy at Muirfield, Jack decided to play a careful game. He played steadily the first three rounds to score even par. But this was not good enough. The weather had turned bright, and Jack found himself six shots behind the brilliant shooting of Lee Trevino.

Driving rains and gusty winds made for poor
playing conditions as Nicklaus teed off on
the first hole of the 1972 British Open.

On the last day Jack attacked the course with all the power of his strong game. A crowd of 20,000 Britons cheered madly as he equaled the course record of 66. At one point he actually led the tournament by one stroke. Still he couldn't hold it. Six times while playing the late holes he had good chances for birdies, but the putts just wouldn't drop in.

Watched by his British fans, Jack prepares to drive off into the wind.

Lee Trevino went ahead to finish with 278. Jack's 279 put him in second place.

Jack was disappointed that he had lost his chance for a Slam that year, but he never lost sight of his real goal. He wanted to be the best golfer the world had ever seen.

He closed out 1972 as if to prove it. He won the Walt Disney World Open with a 267, 21 strokes under par. It was the best tournament performance of the year. Again he set a record for money winnings. He collected $320,542. With this sum he surpassed Arnold Palmer's record for lifetime winnings from golf. Jack's total was now $1,703,705.

Jack Nicklaus never stops working on his game. The next year he hit some bad shots in the Masters, so he had to practice harder for the Tournament of Champions. He came back with a strong game to nose out Lee Trevino for that title by one stroke.

In August of 1973 Jack finally surpassed

Bobby Jones's great record of thirteen major titles. Jack won the P.G.A. tournament by four strokes. Now his total of major titles had reached fourteen, one more than Jones.

By the end of 1973 Jack also became the first golfer ever to win two million dollars in prize money. In 1974 he was one of the first eleven golfing greats elected to the new Golf Hall of Fame.

Jack knows how hard it is to hold on to the perfect touch, even for those who make the game a profession. Though the competition gets more fierce every year, Jack intends to win more tournaments—big and little—than anyone. He has the self-discipline and iron will to keep himself going when the playing becomes rough.

Even when he isn't winning all the big ones, Jack Nicklaus insists the life of a tournament golfer is wonderful. And to prove it he has written a book called *The*

Greatest Game of All. This book tells what it has meant to Jack to spend his life playing golf. It is the exciting life story of the "Golden Bear."

Jack has followed the traditional path to golfing fame, by way of an expert teacher and family backing. What sets him apart is his determination to perfect his game—to do everything better than anyone else. Because he is so serious, Jack has fewer enthusiastic fans than some of the other leaders. But his great ability has won the respect and admiration of everyone who knows and understands the game of golf.

Before his career is over, Jack hopes to prove himself the greatest golfer of them all, by setting records no one can reach.

Lee Trevino
Super Mex

A buzz of excitement ran through the crowd gathered at the first tee of the Merion Golf Club at Ardmore, Pennsylvania. It was June 21, 1971. The United States Open golf championship was about to be decided.

Jack Nicklaus and Lee Trevino had tied for the lead after the regular 72 holes had been played. Now they were set to play an extra 18 holes for the championship.

Husky Jack sat at the edge of the tee. He was waiting to tee off. Jack looked very serious as he thought about the match ahead of him.

The tournament officials were talking in whispers about last-minute details. Among them were the highest officers of the United States Golf Association.

Short, chunky Lee Trevino looked over his clubs as he waited. The round-faced, dark-haired man pulled at the baseball cap for which he was famous. The waiting made Lee restless. Why was everyone so serious? Golf was supposed to be fun.

Jack Nicklaus looked up and saw something strange in Lee's golf bag. He motioned to Lee and pointed at the bag. Lee gave a mischievous grin. He reached into his golf bag and pulled out a long green snake—a rubber snake. Lee tossed it across to Jack Nicklaus.

Jack jumped up and caught the snake, then he burst out laughing. Lee joined in, slapping his thigh.

The tournament officials were startled.

What kind of foolishness was this at such an important moment? Most of the spectators joined in the laughter.

"Oh, that Trevino!" said a man standing nearby. "Anything for a laugh!"

"Until he's ready to hit the ball, you mean," added his neighbor. "He does that clowning to relax."

The man was right. Lee laughed and joked and talked. "Five years ago I was teeing my ball on a dirt mound," he said. "Today I've got tees with my name on them."

Then it was time to tee off. Lee was suddenly serious.

He set his ball just right on the wooden tee. He took his driver from the caddie. Quickly he set himself, ready to swing. All his attention was centered on the ball. He looked down the fairway once, settled his club in position behind the ball, and swung.

There was a *swish* as the club whistled through the air and a *crack* as the clubhead met the ball. In a long, low-rising flight, the ball soared beautifully down the fairway. It rolled into good position for Lee's next shot.

"Oh, nice shot!" exclaimed a delighted spectator. The crowd buzzed until Jack Nicklaus stepped up to drive.

Jack took longer to set his powerful frame for his drive. Then he got off one of his tremendous shots, high and far.

"How can he do it?" exclaimed a fan. "His ball is way past Trevino's."

"Just you wait," said a friend. "Trevino's in plenty good position."

As the players strode down the fairway, Lee was smiling, talking, joking again, with Jack, with the caddies, with the crowd. Win or lose, Lee Trevino intended to enjoy playing golf that day. He liked a challenge,

Lee Trevino shares a handshake and a joke with Jack Nicklaus at the 1971 U.S. Open.

Trevino fired a 68 in the play-off round of the 1971 U.S. Open to defeat Nicklaus and win the trophy.

and he was playing against the man he considered the toughest competitor in golf.

Lee met the challenge by playing some great golf. He scored a 68 to Jack's 71. Happy Lee Trevino became United States Open champion for the second time in the four years he had been on the professional tour.

Lee Trevino has confidence in his game

even though he has what he calls a "bad swing." It is more like a baseball swing than a classic golf swing. He taught himself to play golf. His self-teaching shows up in this unusual swing.

Lee Buck Trevino was born in Dallas, Texas, on December 1, 1939. He never knew his father. His mother, Juanita, worked to support him in his early years. They lived with his grandfather, Joe Trevino, a gravedigger. Their home, a four-room frame house with no electricity and no running water, was in the country just outside of Dallas. It stood in a hayfield far from neighbors, next to the cemetery where Joe worked and next to the Glen Lakes Country Club.

As a boy, Lee had no friends his own age. He had very little money to spend. He played basketball with a tennis ball; he made a football from a taped tin can. Then he learned to find lost golf balls near the club course and sell them back to the players. He put together two rake handles and a chicken-wire scoop to fish balls out of the water hazards. He soon had a small but steady income.

Lee got his first golf club when he was only six. He found an old wooden-shafted five-iron and sawed it off to fit him. Then he started to hit any round object in sight. Before long he got tired of make-believe, so he made a two-hole course in the pasture. When the hay was cut in the summertime, he had a fine course of his own. He played putting games with his grandfather.

Lee left school in the eighth grade to work for the greenskeeper at the Glen Lakes club. He was on the maintenance crew. Lee also sometimes caddied. When the club members finished playing at dusk, he had a chance to play a few holes. But at this time he took no serious interest in the game.

Lee's life changed when he was seventeen. He joined the marines and was sent to Japan. He loved being a marine. He and the other marines had fun together, and Lee was lively and well liked. He was enjoying life. When he found the Third Marine Division had a golf team, he was even happier. He became a member of the team by shooting a brilliant 66 in a try-out. For two years he entered tournaments in Japan, Formosa, and the Philippines. They were mostly just fun to him, but he usually finished toward the top. He really became serious about golf when he re-enlisted and was sent to Okinawa. There he played with high-ranking officers and beat them. In time he was promoted to the rank of sergeant. He also worked to improve his golf game.

Lee returned to Dallas in 1961 and spent a lot of time playing at the Tenison Park municipal golf course. He would show up at the course without shoes, dressed in cut-off Bermuda shorts and a sloppy shirt. He carried an old canvas golf bag over his shoulder. He looked like anything but an expert golfer. Everyone he played thought they could beat him. But Lee says he never lost a game. Just for fun he often played with only one club, a three-iron. Sometimes he would challenge players to an obstacle course where they would shoot across the railroad tracks, down a gravel road, through a tunnel, and then back onto the course.

Soon Lee was making his living by running Hardy's Greenwood Pitch-N-Putt par-three course. Crowds would gather to see him hit the ball with a soft-drink bottle. It was usually a quart-sized bottle wrapped with adhesive tape so it would have a good hitting surface. Lee had to bend way over to hit the ball, but he could drive it 150 yards with the bottle. He could make the ball hit a tree at that distance almost every time. He putted using the bottle like a cue stick. In his room at night he would practice hitting short shots with a golf club. He hit the ball off the bare floor into a shoe on the shelf.

Lee entered and won many local tournaments. He gave lessons and practiced hard as he became more and more devoted to golf. In the summer of 1964, he was married. Soon Lee became an assistant pro at the Horizon Hills Golf Club in El Paso, Texas. He and his wife Claudia lived in a trailer four miles from the course, and Lee jogged to work to keep his legs in shape. It was at Horizon City that Lee decided to work seriously to become a great golfer.

Lee had to perfect his game on the scrubby, heat-baked fairways of the Horizon Hills course. Sand-filled winds often blew as hard as 60 miles an hour. But that didn't stop Lee. He put on scuba-diving goggles to protect his eyes, and he learned to hit the ball low, to keep it out of the powerful gusts of wind.

Lee had an unusual way of standing. Instead of facing the ball squarely, he pulled back his left foot. It was a very "open" stance, usually used for short shots or special shots. Still, it was a good style for him, because it made his swing more powerful when the clubhead met the ball. His swing was compact, flat, and choppy. He sent his drives off the tee like a baseball player hitting sharp singles to center. His shots were not extra-long, but he made up for lack of distance by placing his shots with great accuracy.

70

This sequence shows Trevino's forceful drive.

He learned to putt as straight and true as an expert shooting a billiard ball.

Lee entered and won the 1965 Texas Open tournament. After this win, the club pro loaned him money for airplane fare to the 1966 U.S. Open. Lee had a poor set of clubs and finished 54th. Discouraged, he refused to enter the 1967 Open, but his wife sent in his registration. He made the best qualifying score and finished fifth in the tournament. For this he won $6,000 and was later named professional Rookie of the Year. He stayed on the professional tournament tour and became a consistent money winner, though he did not win a tournament until the following year. In 1968, after finishing second at Houston and at Atlanta, he won a big prize. Like Jack Nicklaus before him, Lee captured his first tournament victory in the U.S. Open.

It was a smashing victory. In winning

the Open at Oak Hill in Rochester, New York, Lee was the first man to play all four rounds under par in the 68 years of Open play. With his scores of 69, 68, 69, 69 for 275, he won countless admirers.

In just one year's time, the bubbling, talkative Trevino became a big favorite. Smiling, walking with a determined stride, and carrying a coin which he said brought him good luck, he charmed the galleries. He was a special hero to the golfers who practice at driving ranges and play golf on municipal courses. He seemed just like one of them—the clerks, the truck drivers, the workingmen who love golf but have little time and money for the game. They admired his success, and he talked to them as friends.

Like Arnold Palmer, Lee had a crowd of loyal fans who followed him around the course at every tournament. Once he turned

Lee and his caddie stride toward the next important shot.

to the crowd and said, "Arnie's got his army, and I've got mine. You're called Lee's Fleas."

Though some of the professionals thought he overdid it, Lee's wisecracking certainly brought the spectators to watch him. They knew that he was serious about golf, but they liked his sense of humor. Lee liked to have fun and win money too. He does both because of his "stay loose" way of thinking.

At the same time he is a hard worker. When he talks about winning he always tells about the hard work that is necessary. He wants all young golfers to get that message.

On the pro tour Lee would skip rope and hit golf balls in his spare time to keep in shape. On the day before the 1968 Masters, he played 36 practice holes and 9 holes on a pitch-and-putt. Then, after a shower, he

A party of Lee's "Fleas." These loyal fans root for Lee at every tournament.

ended at midnight on a par-three course, playing another 9 holes in a sports coat and alligator shoes. Prior to the British Open, he spent eight full days hitting 600 to 700 balls a day. He was learning to hit the smaller British ball. "You've got to hit the ball in this game until your hands bleed," he said.

After winning the 1968 U.S. Open, he went on to win the Hawaiian Open and a total of $132,000 for the year. In 1969 he won the Tucson Open, the World Cup Individual prize, and over $100,000.

In 1970 his only wins were early in the year, but he was pleased that he won the "triple crown": First, he was the leading money winner, with $157,037. Second, he led in the Exemption Point standings that qualify players for the tournaments. Third, he won the Vardon Trophy for the lowest scoring average in all the professional tournaments. However, after winning the Tucson Open in Arizona and the National Airlines Open in Miami, Florida, in a play-off, he did not win again for thirteen months. Now he was not always so care-free. He became nervous and tried to do too many different things. His golf game went into a slump. He attended too many banquets, made too many speeches, and got into too many businesses on the side. He even dropped out of several tournaments in despair over his slump.

Still he did not lose his sense of humor. At the British Open in 1970, he was intro-duced to the prime minister of Great Britain. Lee grinned and stuck out his hand. "Ever shake hands with a Mexican before?" he asked.

Lee is proud to be a Mexican-American. He often calls himself the Mex. He is proud, too, of his struggle to overcome poverty. And he doesn't mind making jokes about it.

Still very nervous about his game, Lee appeared at an exhibition in Palm Beach, Florida, early in 1971. Jack Nicklaus told him that he was good enough to beat the best. This comment seemed to snap Trevino out of his slump. He cut down on his outside activities. He concentrated on golf. In April 1971 he won the Tallahassee Open. This win started him off on a fiery winning streak. In this burst of great golf playing, Trevino took the giant step from "good" to "great." He became a superstar.

The next step in his streak toward success was the 1971 U.S. Open. It was there that he carried his green rubber snake and beat Nicklaus in the play-off. Lee followed this win by taking first in the Canadian Open. He did it in a sensational way. He was behind by three strokes starting the

Whether hitting one out of the rough (above) or sinking one on the green, Lee shows the skill that won him the Canadian Open in 1971 and $30,000 in prize money.

seventeenth hole in the final round. Lee played the hole at two under par by sinking a 105-yard wedge shot for an eagle. He made a 35-foot putt on the last hole to tie for the lead. This took him into a play-off—which he won.

When interviewed by reporters after winning the Canadian Open, Lee said his goal, besides winning tournaments, was to win a million dollars.

Then he went to the British Open. Here he won his third big title in 20 days. Lee was the first to win these three titles in a single year.

In the British Open Tony Jacklin was the local favorite. Some of Tony's fans were so eager for him to win that they even booed Lee. That made Lee want to win all the more. As his lead increased, Lee was shouting encouragement to himself. On his last round Trevino put his ball in the cup from 10 feet on the first hole, 20 feet on the third, and 16 feet on the fourth. All were for birdies. On the sixth hole, from the blind side of a ridge, he shot with his three-wood into the unknown.

Lee shouted something.

"What did he say?" inquired a spectator.

"He said, 'It looks perfect—I just hope it goes far enough!'"

When Lee crossed the ridge, he found he had hit the ball 270 yards. It was lying on the green, three feet from the cup.

Lee carried a five-stroke lead halfway through the final day. Then he took a very bad 7 on the next-to-last hole. Still he won with a birdie 4 on the eighteenth. He had a 70 for the round and a total of 278, just one stroke less than Lu Liang-huan of Taiwan.

Lee was overcome with joy after holing the winning putt. He sank to his knees. He was so happy he held his face in his hands.

Back home in El Paso, Texas, Lee is mobbed by fans as he rides with his family.

He lay flat on the ground for a moment before springing to his feet.

Lee got $13,200 for his victory, a small purse by American standards. Nevertheless he sat down and wrote a check for $4,800 to a local orphanage. He "wanted to do something for the kids like me who had a difficult start in life."

This was not unusual for Lee. After the 1968 Hawaiian Open he put $10,000 into a trust fund for the children of an Hawaiian pro who had been accidentally killed. In 1969 he donated his World Cup purse of $2,000 to a caddie scholarship fund in Singapore. After the 1971 Memphis Open he gave $5,000 from his first prize to Saint Jude's Hospital. He also works hard helping other charities, like Christmas Seals and Easter Seals, the Boys Club, and the Shriners in El Paso.

Around El Paso in the summer of 1971, Lee became a great hero, especially to the many Mexican-Americans who lived there. There was even a song written about him. Some of the words were "Long live Lee Trevino the Super-Mexican." So his nickname became "Super-Mex." He used a sombrero as an emblem on his baseball-type cap. On the newsstands his pictures seemed to be everywhere. He was heard on radio. He appeared in exhibition matches, which

Lee breaks the tension of professional competition with jokes, tricks, and laughter.

were often shown on television. The sight of Lee, tossing his cap, swinging a club, laughing, joking, became familiar and welcome to his many new friends.

As he became more famous, Lee began to endorse commercial products and to invest in different businesses. He also made golf instruction films for television.

"I try to be funny out on the course," says Lee. "It's my way of putting something back into the game. I can't put back the money—I've spent it all."

Off he goes, teeing up and talking, talking, talking. "You only go round once in life"—*thwack*, he hits the ball—"and you gotta smell the roses as you go by."

Lee loves to brag about his exhibition appearances. He says he shoots eighteen holes for good money, and in return the customers get plenty of golf and fun as well.

"The only time I stop yakking is when I'm asleep," he tells everyone.

After his great year in 1971, what would Trevino do next? The year 1972 started shaping up as a Nicklaus year. Jack won the Masters and the Open in great style. It looked as if Nicklaus could become the first to win the British Open and the P.G.A. to complete the Grand Slam.

Instead, Lee Trevino slammed the door on Jack in dramatic fashion. At the British Open Nicklaus and Tony Jacklin were the favorites. But Trevino's play was dazzling. He delighted the galleries with his bubbling mixture of nonstop chatter, supreme confidence, and good luck. He burst into the lead with an all but unbelievable streak of five straight birdies at the end of the third round. He holed out *four* shots from off the greens—an almost impossible feat!

Here's what he did: First, on the second

day, he sank a 40-foot eight-iron chip shot for a birdie three at the second hole. Second, after making birdies at fourteen and fifteen in his third round, he seemed to be in great trouble at the sixteenth hole. He had a bad lie—up against the bank of a bunker. He slammed his wedge into the sand. The ball spurted out, a semi-line drive headed far over the green. But the fast moving ball took one bounce and banged *smack* into the cup for a birdie two. It was an unbelievable sight.

Even Lee admitted he should have made a four or a five! Third, at eighteen, he chipped out of the weeds right into the cup for his fifth straight birdie.

Fourth, the real pay off came at the seventeenth hole of the final round. Tony Jacklin, fighting for the lead and playing with Trevino, was just off the green in two. He chipped his third shot fifteen feet from the cup, giving him a good chance for a birdie four.

Lee drove into a bunker. He poked the ball out short on his second shot. His next shot was short of the green. His fourth ran across the green into the rough.

There was Jacklin, with a chance for a four, and Trevino seemed certain to make six, maybe seven or eight. Instead, Lee chipped his ball out of the rough and right into the cup for a par five.

It made Jacklin so nervous that he took *three* putts for a six! He had lost a stroke instead of gaining several and going ahead. Lee made his par on the last hole for his 278 and victory. Nicklaus closed strong to slip into second place, and Jacklin fell to third.

Lee was sorry to beat Jack Nicklaus—but he had come to England to win! He now had his second British Open title to go with

A chip shot onto the green during the 1972 British Open brings out the serious side of Lee and his fans.

his two U.S. Open wins in five years on the professional tour.

Sore muscles bothered Lee in 1973. Still he won smashing victories in two big tournaments, the Inverarry and the Doral in Florida.

In 1973 he also achieved one of the goals of his golfing career. He passed the million dollar mark in total winnings.

His career shows that a man of talent and determination can come from nowhere and reach the top in golf.

For all his chattering Lee studies his game and the courses constantly. He measures the distances of hazards from the greens the way Nicklaus does. He knows just how far he can hit the ball with any given club. He has refined his style of play. He still can hit low line drives, but now he can also hit high, booming shots like those of Nicklaus. He takes pride in his ability to fade his shots just right—and thus control them. Now he has a better mixture of shots. He once refused to enter the Masters because his low shots didn't roll well there. Now he fears nothing.

Learning and confidence made the difference between the earlier good player and the star who emerged in 1971.

"Trevino is the greatest player today because of his hands," says the old master Ben Hogan. "He uses them beautifully."

Of course he still sometimes hits a bad shot. Then he gets angry and blames the caddie.

"Getting mad is what drives you to come back after your mistakes," he says. He lets off steam so that he is relaxed for the next shot.

Lee plays the way he lives, fast and hard and joyously. He thinks that's the way golf should be approached.

Lee Trevino was honored as Sportsman of the Year in 1971 by *Sports Illustrated* magazine, for his great performance and for adding the flavor of joy to his sport. He has won many other awards, too, such as the Hickock Belt for great sports achievement. The Associated Press named him Athlete of the Year for 1971.

Lee has always insisted that his goal is to have fun playing golf and to make a good living at the same time. He stands high on the list of all-time money winners, and anyone who has seen him play knows what a good time he has on the golf course.

But Lee works hard too to keep his great skill sharp—a skill that should enable him to challenge any golfer anywhere for some time to come.

One thing is sure: it will be a long time before anyone comes along who can surpass Trevino as golf's most exciting player and most colorful personality. That day may *never* come!

On August 12, 1974 these two great pros—Jack Nicklaus and Lee Trevino—went into the final round of the P.G.A. tournament, fighting hard for first place.

"I'm going all out to win!" declared Lee Trevino. He led by a single stroke after 54 holes at the Tanglewood course in Clemmons, North Carolina.

Seldom had there been such a close finish in a major tournament. The leaders, Nicklaus and Trevino, were being pressed hard by other players. But as the final 18 holes progressed, the contest settled down to a fight between the two men.

As they stood on the 18th tee, Lee Trevino was still one shot ahead. Could he hold off Jack's challenge?

Trevino won the 1974 P.G.A. with skill, determination, and his usual good humor.

Nicklaus drove first, a long, carefully placed shot. Lee Trevino stepped up and smacked his drive even farther out.

There was a roar from the crowd.

Jack Nicklaus lofted a beautiful iron shot to the 18th green, just 20 feet from the cup. Then Lee sent his approach shot even closer to the cup.

Now it was up to Jack to try for a birdie to catch Lee. Jack aimed his putt carefully, stroked the ball well. The crowd gasped as the ball slid just past the cup to one side.

Lee Trevino could win if he used only two putts. He rolled his first putt very close to the hole. He tapped in his second, and he had his title. He had won the P.G.A. for the first time in his career!

Lee raised his hand joyfully, and his face broke into a dazzling smile.

Jack Nicklaus just shook his head. Even in losing, though, he had set another record. He had come in second for the twelfth time in a major tournament. And for the twenty-sixth time, he had come in first or second!

Trevino was the victor this time, but one thing was certain: Lee and Jack would meet again at tournaments still to come. And when they do, it's anyone's guess as to which one of these two golfing greats will come out on top.

A Golfing Glossary

approach shot: a shot that is intended to reach the putting green

birdie: one stroke under par at any given hole

chip shot: a short approach shot with low flight

drive: the first shot on any hole, often hit with a driver or other wooden-headed club

eagle: two strokes under par at any given hole

fade: the course of a ball in flight when it curves gently to the right

fairway: a grassy area extending from tee to putting green

green or **putting green:** close-cropped grassy area where a cup is placed

hazard: a sand trap, bunker, ditch, or body of water

hole: the actual hole or cup where a golfer must hit his ball. Also, one of the eighteen divisions of a golf course, covering the stretch from tee to green.

hole out: to finish putting, or to knock the ball into the cup from anywhere

hook: the course of a ball in flight when it curves to the left. When it curves sharply it is called a **duck hook.**

iron: any one of several clubs with a metal head, used for shorter and more accurate shots than wood clubs

lie: the position of a ball on the ground

par: the perfect score at each hole of a golf course. This score is determined by the length of the hole.

pitch shot: a short approach shot with arched flight

punch shot: a low-flying shot made by striking down at the ball

putt: a light stroke made on the putting green, aimed at getting the ball into the cup

slice: the course of a ball in flight when it curves sharply to the right

stroke: each time a player hits or attempts to hit the ball, it counts as a stroke.

The Augusta National Golf Course

Tournament golf is played on eighteen-hole courses similar to the Augusta National Golf Course shown here. This is where the Masters tournament takes place each year.

This invitational tournament is one of four that make up the Pro Grand Slam. Like all professional tournaments, it is scored on the basis of four rounds, or 72 holes.

Augusta has a par 72 for eighteen holes. The par for a hole is determined by its length. If the distance from tee to cup is 250 yards or less, the par is 3. For a distance between 251 and 470 yards, the par is set at 4. Any hole longer than 470 yards gets the top rating of par 5.

Championship courses vary in length. Augusta is about 7000 yards long but, like other tournament courses, it changes from year to year. Tees and greens are repositioned frequently in order to make the golf course more challenging.

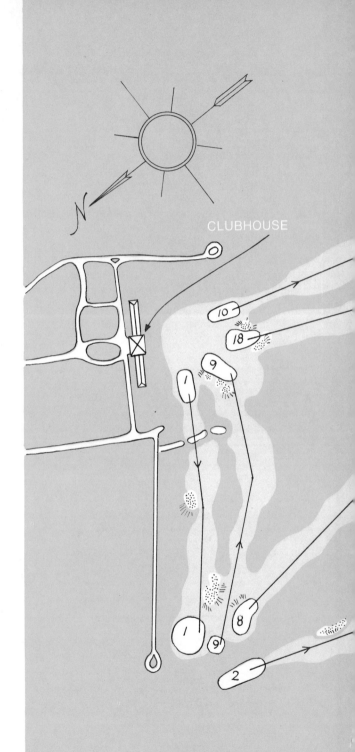

CLUBHOUSE